D1061069

# HISTORIC PHOTOS OF
# TULSA

## TEXT AND CAPTIONS BY JERRY L. CORNELIUS

TURNER
PUBLISHING COMPANY
Nashville, Tennessee   Paducah, Kentucky

The Tulsa skyline in 1962 across the
Sun Refinery tank farm.

# HISTORIC PHOTOS OF
# T U L S A

Turner Publishing Company
200 4th Avenue North • Suite 950        412 Broadway • P.O. Box 3101
Nashville, Tennessee 37219        Paducah, Kentucky 42002-3101
(615) 255-2665        (270) 443-0121

www.turnerpublishing.com

*Historic Photos of Tulsa*

Copyright © 2007 Turner Publishing Company

Library of Congress Control Number: 2007923671

ISBN-13: 978-1-59652-342-5
ISBN: 1-59652-342-5

Printed in the United States of America

07 08 09 10 11 12 13 14—0 9 8 7 6 5 4 3 2 1

# CONTENTS

ACKNOWLEDGMENTS.................................................................VII

PREFACE ...............................................................................VIII

INDIAN TERRITORY
(1882–1904) ....................................................................... 1

OIL BOOM
(1905–1918) ...................................................................... 33

PROSPERITY, RIOT, AND DEPRESSION
(1919–1939) ...................................................................... 63

THE OIL CAPITAL OF THE WORLD
(1940–1972)...................................................................... 131

NOTES ON THE PHOTOGRAPHS .................................................. 200

On the Historic Register, the Golden Driller stands outside the Tulsa fairgrounds' Expo Center. It was originally created for an International Petroleum Exposition show in the 1970s.

# ACKNOWLEDGMENTS

This volume, *Historic Photos of Tulsa,* is the result of the cooperation and efforts of many individuals and organizations. It is with great thanks that we acknowledge the valuable contribution of the following for their generous support:

Beryl Ford Collection
Tulsa City-County Library
Jerry L. Cornelius Collection

We would also like to thank the following individuals for valuable contributions and assistance in making this work possible:

Beryl D. Ford
Chris Lair

# PREFACE

Tulsa has thousands of historic photographs that reside in archives, both locally and nationally. This book began with the observation that, while those photographs are of great interest to many, they are not easily accessible. During a time when Tulsa is looking ahead and evaluating its future course, many people are asking, How do we treat the past? These decisions affect every aspect of the city—architecture, public spaces, commerce, infrastructure—and these, in turn, affect the way that people live their lives. This book seeks to provide easy access to a valuable, objective look into the history of Tulsa.

The power of photographs is that they are less subjective than words in their treatment of history. Although the photographer can make decisions regarding subject matter and how to capture and present it, photographs do not provide the breadth of interpretation that text does. For this reason, they offer an original, untainted perspective that allows the viewer to interpret and observe.

This project represents countless hours of review and research. The researchers and writer have reviewed thousands of photographs in numerous archives. We greatly appreciate the generous assistance of the individuals and organizations listed in the acknowledgments of this work, without whom this project could not have been completed.

The goal in publishing this work is to provide broader access to this set of extraordinary photographs that seek to inspire, provide perspective, and evoke insight that might assist people who are responsible for determining Tulsa's future. In addition, the book seeks to preserve the past with adequate respect and reverence.

With the exception of touching up imperfections caused by the damage of time and cropping where necessary, no other changes have been made. The focus and clarity of many images is limited to the technology and the ability of the photographer at the time they were taken.

The work is divided into eras. Beginning with some of the earliest known photographs of Tulsa, the first section records photographs through the beginning of the twentieth century. The second section spans early years of the twentieth century through World War I. Section 3 moves into the Twenties and the Depression era between the World Wars. The last section covers the World War II era to recent times.

In each of these sections we have made an effort to capture various aspects of life through our selection of photographs. People, commerce, transportation, infrastructure, religious institutions, and educational institutions have been included to provide a broad perspective.

We encourage readers to reflect as they go walking in Tulsa, strolling through the city, its parks, and its neighborhoods. It is the publisher's hope that in utilizing this work, longtime residents will learn something new and that new residents will gain a perspective on where Tulsa has been, so that each can contribute to its future.

*Todd Bottorff, Publisher*

On October 15, 1897, the Tulsa weather appeared to be excellent, as it usually is that time of year, so these young Tulsans went for a bicycle ride. The three women are identified as "miss" and none of the group seems to be married, judging from different last names.

# INDIAN TERRITORY

## (1882–1904)

The United States relocated the Indian tribes from their traditional homelands to what is now known as the State of Oklahoma. The eastern half of the state was called Indian Territory, the western part Oklahoma Territory. The City of Tulsa originally sat in the northern corner of the Creek Nation but expanded into the Cherokee Nation, actually only a few blocks north, and eventually into part of the Osage Nation.

The land was first leased from the Indians and later purchased by white settlers and businessmen. A good deal of the land in present south Tulsa was owned by the Perryman family. Josiah Perryman was the first postmaster. The post office was in his brother's barn and later in an addition to his house before relocating near the railroad depot after mail began arriving by train.

Extremely important to the beginning of Tulsa was the Frisco Railroad, which completed laying track to Tulsa in August 1882. A tent city greeted the workers as they built a station and rail yard before continuing west with a bridge across the Arkansas River. In later years, other railroads were lured to the town thanks to the shrewd vision of local businessmen and commercial promotional organizations. As a result of the efforts of these men, the original Tulsa business area remained the buying center of the area even though the railroad had crossed the river and established other stations.

With the advent of the railroads, Tulsa gained two general merchandise stores (Hall and Archer) and soon had five (Brady, Lynch, and Bynum), along with a hotel and other businesses, all within one block of the tracks. The 1st Presbyterian church and Mission school opened its doors the next year and the Methodist Episcopal church soon thereafter.

Tulsa was incorporated on January 18, 1898. A year later an entire block of downtown was destroyed by fire, prompting the formation of a volunteer fire department, which boasted one horse-drawn wagon.

In 1904, seeing the need for a way for horses, wagons, and people to cross the river, several businessmen formed a corporation and built a privately owned toll bridge, which proved to be extremely valuable to Tulsa after oil was discovered. The county government later purchased the bridge and discontinued the toll.

With oil in its future, Tulsa was on the threshold of unprecedented growth.

A somewhat ragtag group of musicians called the Tulsa Band pose in 1899 in front of the Lewis and Brobeck Hardware store. No record exists of how well they played.

Students and a teacher pose for a group portrait at the Presbyterian Mission school in 1893. The school was the forerunner of the Tulsa public schools, which opened on the same property a decade later.

Onlookers survey the waters from the Frisco Railroad bridge across the Arkansas River during the 1897 flood. Although not intended for pedestrians, it was the only way across the river during a flood. This steel bridge with concrete supports was actually the second Frisco bridge—the first washed out during an earlier flood.

Main and 2nd Street in 1896, facing north on Main. The white building at right housed Scott's General Store on the 1st floor and a hotel on the second. The building with the spire, in the background at right, is the 1st National Bank. On December 5, 1897, this side of the street burned down except for one stone building.

A small residence at 202 South Maybelle (ca. 1890s).

More than 3,000 head of cattle are being fed near what is now Pine and Cincinnati. They had been driven from Missouri and await shipment on one of Tulsa's railroads. The men are, from left, Hank Guilfold and Sig Crowder on horses, Rabbit Harris, John Cox, Lon Swazey, C. H. Hinton, and V. I. Shirtleff.

Tulsa from "Standpipe Hill" in 1892. The white church on the right eventually became the 1st Methodist church.

Thomas J. Archer's first general merchandise store at 1st and Main in 1893. Archer is standing on the porch in the white shirt and vest. He would later die inside another of his stores when an intoxicated passerby accidentally fired a pistol from the street at gunpowder kegs stored inside.

Looking north on Main from 2nd Street in 1893. In the building at left, the W. E. Jones Saddlery store and Gillette's Hardware occupy the first floor and the Turner hotel the second. Three men are posing on the roof of the porch.

Tulsa's first unofficial post office was in this barn on the George Perryman farm near 3rd and Lewis. Later, Joshia Perryman was named postmaster, receiving $1.50 a month. After the Frisco railroad established a depot, the mail was delivered to Tulsa by train and the post office was moved to "downtown" Tulsa.

J. M. Hall was a major influence in Tulsa in the early years. He is shown here in front of his store (white shirt on left) in 1894. J. M. and his brother opened a store in Tulsa in 1882. The brother died a few years later. Hall's store sold numerous items including groceries and furniture. The small sign nailed to the far left porch post advertises "salt."

The interior of the T. J. Archer store in 1892. The gunpowder kegs caused Archer's death when a stray bullet exploded the powder. A wood-burning cook stove is for sale in the center of the store.

Tulsa's first mayor,
Colonel Edward Calkins.

The Palace Market displays meat and hides (ca. 1890s).

One way to cross the Arkansas River before the first pedestrian bridge was completed in 1904 was on this cable ferry.

The east side of Main Street in 1895. The Frisco Meat Market in the building to the left advertises "cash paid for hides."

The Arthur F. Antle Livery Barn was built in 1894.

The Presbyterian Mission school near 4th and Boston in 1893.

A paddle-wheel ferry crosses the Arkansas River in 1896. In the distance beyond, a herd of cattle is being driven across. When the river was too high, cattle could not be driven to the other side, and when it was too low, the ferry could not operate.

Three onlookers at rooftop survey the rubble following
the Main Street fire of 1897.

Shown here is Tulsa's first telephone company in 1901. Owner Robert Hall, son of Tulsa pioneer H. C. Hall, stands behind the operator. This Indian Nations telephone company became Pioneer Telephone, and around 1918, Southwestern Bell.

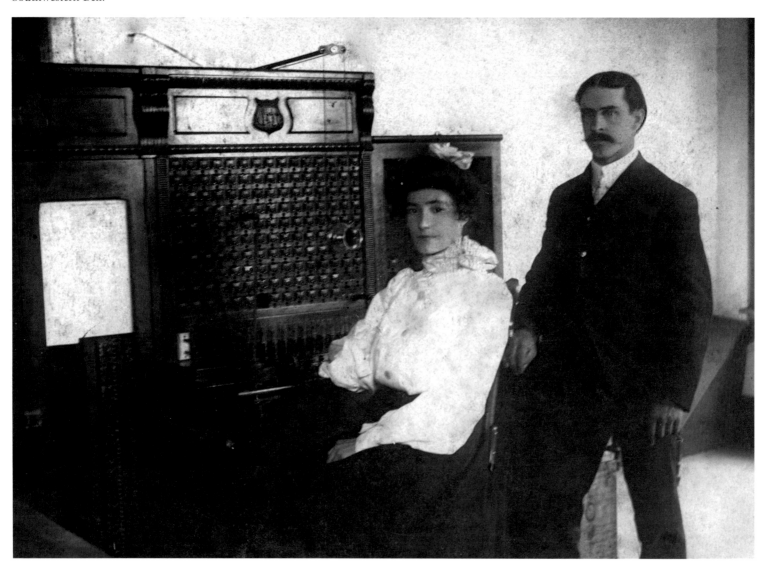

The first Tulsa hospital took care of patients here on West 5th Street.
A horse-drawn ambulance and a nurse pose for the camera.

An advocate for the Woman's Christian Temperance Union (WCTU) in early Tulsa, Lilah Lindsey campaigned against the ill effects of alcohol abuse on the family and society.

Two of the most famous Wild West show operators, Pawnee Bill and Buffalo Bill, hold a powwow. The Pawnee Bill museum is near Tulsa.

A crowd convenes at the Frisco Railroad depot (ca. 1900).

A group in the lobby of the Alcorn Hotel poses for the camera. A sign on the back wall advertises sending clothing out to be cleaned and pressed. A wood-burning stove at left provides heating for lobby staff and guests.

The first oil well in Tulsa, the Sue Bland #1, began pumping in 1901 in the Red Fork area of West Tulsa. It did not prove to be a large oil field, but it did attract wildcatters, who eventually discovered an important oil field, Glenn Pool, only four years later.

A Tulsa residence at 6th and Cheyenne (ca. 1900).

A 1903 skyline view of Tulsa, facing south from Standpipe Hill. The hill is about six blocks north of the Frisco tracks on Cincinnati and was called "standpipe" because of a water tower erected at the site.

Inside the Tulsa Banking Company in 1903. From left are A. F. Herndon, Miss Vona Clay, Charles W. Brown, and W. R. Ritchie behind the teller's window. The company may still rely on gas lighting but has entered the twentieth century with an electric fan.

Woodward Park at 21st and Lewis.

# OIL BOOM

## (1905–1918)

In 1901, oil was discovered in the Red Fork area of West Tulsa. The well was called the Sue Bland #1. Although not the first well in Oklahoma, it did attract wildcat oil men, who combed the landscape for more sites.

Four years later, two of them were successful. Robert Galbreath and Frank Chelsey obtained a lease about 10 miles southwest of Tulsa. They hit a gusher on November 22, 1905, calling it Ida Glenn #1 for the Creek Indian woman who owned the property. With its railroads, all-weather bridge, and commerce center, Tulsa was prepared for this watershed moment. A period of startling growth enveloped the city. From an estimated population of 1,390 in 1900, the number of residents by 1920 had leaped to 72,075, and nearly doubled again only ten years later.

Oklahoma is well known for the land runs of the late nineteenth century; but all these runs were in Oklahoma Territory, the western half of the territory that would become the state. Tulsa was in Indian Territory in the east. After a series of government manipulations, the land was finally parceled out to individual members of the Indian tribes calling the land home.

Business owners with stores and buildings on Indian land were supposed to buy the land they occupied from the tribes. The reported value of this downtown Tulsa land was several million dollars, but when the deals were done, the tribes had sold the land for a few hundred thousand dollars.

Tulsa's growth was not without its growing pains, not the least of which was water, at least good water. Tulsa was getting its drinking water from the Arkansas River. A dozen or more refineries were dumping waste into the river, and the water was not fit for man or animal. Finding another water supply was not difficult but developing it into a city water system was a topic of great debate between 1910 and 1920. The completion of the Spavinaw Water Project, from a lake 70 miles to the east, would solve the problem in the next decade.

With all the benefits Tulsa was receiving from the oil industry, there was not one oil well in the city. Tulsans loved their oil but didn't want to see it or especially smell it. They passed a law early on that forbade drilling inside the city.

The oil discovery that made Tulsa a great oil center for the next 75 years was Glenn Pool. The discovery well, Ida Glenn #1, was named after the Creek woman on whose land the well was drilled. There was so much oil, it was pumped into earth pits, such as this one, until tanks and pipelines could be built. A good deal of oil was lost storing it in this manner.

A typical Tulsa residence early in the century at 402 South Lansing, the eastern edge of Tulsa.

Street-paving teams at 2nd and Maybelle line up for a
photograph ca. 1909.

A band that toured the country promoting Tulsa poses in front of the State, War, and Navy Building in Washington, D.C., on April 17, 1908. The sign reads, "Tulsa, Oklahoma, Age 6 Yrs, Pop 16,300; 5 railroads; Resources: oil and gas, coal, cement, cotton, corn, alfalfa, wheat." Tulsa actually had incorporated 10 years earlier, not six, as the sign indicates.

The Frisco Railroad depot was located between Main and Boston. This building was later enlarged. Early Tulsa merchants were able to get the Frisco to build their station here because the area was part of the Creek Indian Nation. The Creeks had a more favorable business policy than the Cherokees, whose territory began just a few blocks north (1905).

The T. J. Archer residence at 510 North Main Street in 1906. Archer ran a general merchandise store in early Tulsa. On the porch are Annie Archer, left, and her mother, Hannah Elizabeth Mowbray. Her father, George W. Mowbray, Sr., who sits in the carriage, was a Methodist minister and later served as mayor of Tulsa.

The first foot bridge across the Arkansas River just after completion in 1904 was a privately owned toll bridge. The sign on the steel beam at the top says, "They said it couldn't be done but we did," referring to the governmental red tape required to obtain permission to build the bridge.

The original Brady Hotel, the two-story building on the right, was completed in 1905. Seven stories were later added and billed as "fire proof." A tea garden was located on the roof, and the two structures were connected by a large pass-through. When the original building caught fire in 1935, it also ignited the newer building, which was not as fireproof as thought.

Main Street on a rainy day ca. 1909. Tulsa was incorporated as a city in 1898. At statehood, in November 1907, an estimated 7,200 residents called the city home. The U.S. census in 1910 listed Tulsa with 18,240 people.

The Woman's Christian Temperance Union holds a meeting ca. 1910. The WCTU was at the forefront of a nationwide movement that led to the Volstead Act prohibiting the sale and manufacture of alcoholic beverages in the United States from 1920 to 1933—the era of Prohibition.

Streetcar rails run the street in 1907.

The Hotel Tulsa at 3rd and Cincinnati, now the site of the Tulsa Performing Arts Center. The hotel was built in 1912, shown here a few years later before three additional floors were added. It is said that more oil deals were made in the lobby of this hotel than any other place in the nation.

Tulsa's finest in 1910. Patrol officers wore London-style "bobbie" hats.

The interior of Shackle's drugstore in 1912. A brass spittoon next to the marble soda fountain sits on the floor, which is composed of carefully laid individual tiles.

A family outing on a day ca. 1910.

A modern print shop ca. 1910. With one electric light, type was set one letter at a time from the cases next to the woman's left hand.

Tulsa's first Boy Scout troop in 1910.

This is the first ladder fire wagon in Tulsa (ca. 1910). Chief Rolla C. Alder is standing at left, followed by Wes Bush, C. T. Bradshaw, and George Jenkins. The horses are named Dan and Joe. The outfit has stopped in front of Tulsa High School on the city block bordered by 4th and 5th streets and by Boston and Cincinnati. Tulsa sold the last of its horses and wagons by 1915 to become a completely mechanized department.

Mrs. Ed. G. Fike and sister Mattie Lou Dischler pose on Tulsa's first pedestrian bridge across the Arkansas River on September 23, 1910. The bridge had been purchased by Tulsa County in 1909.

On a January 27, the East End Cafe has seating at the counter for eight and serves "hot wafels." On other back-wall signs, the cafe claims to be "fair to organized labor," and Dick Bardon offers to make loans "on all goods of value."

To promote Tulsa ca. 1905 to 1910, the city sent traveling delegations to many eastern cities. This one was photographed in Terre Haute, Indiana, in March 1905. The man kneeling near the center of the photo in a white shirt is humorist Will Rogers.

This 3-chair barbershop sports electrical wiring and ornate barber chairs.
A sign on the mirror defines it as a "union shop."

Originally housing all grades, this building was later the home of Tulsa High School. It was located in the city block from 4th to 5th streets, from Boston to Cincinnati, also the location of the Presbyterian Mission school before 1900. The school moved to 6th and Cincinnati in 1917 and was renamed Central High School.

Third Street east from Boulder in 1910. The Tulsa
World building is at far left.

The YMCA building was built in 1912 at the corner of 4th and Cincinnati across the street from "old" City Hall. The YMCA moved to a new facility at 6th and Denver in the early 1950s. One of the projects undertaken to raise money for the new building was selling Lifesaver candy, five rolls for a quarter. A multi-story parking garage has stood on this site for more than 50 years.

A group of young adults pose on the Arkansas River bridge ca. 1910. Since Tulsa had few cars during the era, many residents walked, drove wagons, or rode horses over the bridge.

War preparations under way, this parade moving south on Main Street in 1917 encourages young men to enlist in the Army. The photograph was made from the Robinson Hotel.

To aid the World War I war effort, the citizens of Tulsa raised and equipped an ambulance company. That group poses outside the Kurhaus Restaurant in Nevenahr, Germany, following the end of the war.

A residential neighborhood in West Tulsa during the 1917 flood.

# Prosperity, Riot, and Depression

## (1919–1939)

World War I was over and Tulsa was still on the move. Buildings were still going up rapidly. Prosperity was everywhere, especially if one were in the oil business.

Central High School, opened in 1917, had to be expanded in 1922. The city library had a new building in 1915, and the fire department was completely mechanized that year. The Rotary Club was also established in 1915.

The original bridge across the Arkansas River was replaced with a concrete and steel structure in 1916, which would be expanded to handle greater volumes of traffic in the mid 1930s.

The Majestic Theater opened in 1918 to show movies, followed by the Rialto and Ritz by 1926. The Orpheum opened in 1924 as a vaudeville theater but began showing movies in 1929.

After years of operating as the *Tulsa Democrat,* the newspaper was purchased by Richard Lloyd Jones in 1919, who changed the name to the *Tulsa Tribune.* Published for more than 70 years, the afternoon paper finally closed its doors in 1992. Only the *Tulsa World,* operated by the Lorton family most of its years, has survived to pass its 100th birthday.

In addition to oil, aviation was a leading contributor to Tulsa's economy. In 1928, supported by the guarantee of several noted Tulsans headed by oil millionaire W. G. Skelly, the first airport opened at Apache and Sheridan, and is still part of the airport's property. Just after opening, Tulsa's airport became the busiest in the country, carrying oil executives aloft who could afford the expensive transportation.

Tulsa began another wave of building in 1926, which ended with the start of the Great Depression. As a result of this and the preceding boom, Tulsa boasted 37 buildings more than 10 stories tall and two more than 20 stories. Among them were the Mayo Hotel (1925), Sinclair (1919), 1st National Bank (1918), 1st Methodist (1922), Masonic building (1922), Adkar Shrine (1925), Exchange Bank expansion (1928), Philtower (1928), Boston Avenue Methodist (1929), Union Depot (1932), Airport Terminal (1932), Will Rogers High School (1939), Skelly Stadium (1930), and the Coliseum (1929).

During the 1920s, the Greenwood District, dubbed nationwide as "Black Wall Street," a flourishing black community made affluent by the oil boom earlier in the century, became a center for jazz and blues culture. A race riot in 1921 burned to the ground thirty-five blocks of the district, and as many as 300 participants, many white, many more black, were killed.

The Great Depression of the 1930s affected everyone, Tulsa included. Crude oil dropped to as low as 10 cents a barrel and the oil business suffered. The population growth Tulsa had experienced since 1905 came to a halt. From 1930 to 1940, the city population increased by fewer than 900.

The Tulsa Library in its first permanent home at 3rd and Cheyenne. The library is now called the Tulsa City-County Library and has 26 locations.

A flood did not keep the deliverymen of Smith's Holsom Bread from making deliveries.

This is Amy Comstock, private secretary to Richard Lloyd Jones, editor and publisher of the *Tulsa Tribune*, in her Tribune building office on the southwest corner of Boston and Archer. Jones came to Tulsa in 1919 and purchased the *Tulsa Democrat* from Charles Page, immediately changing the name to the *Tribune*. The afternoon paper was published daily until 1992.

Lake Yahola, part of the municipal water system at Mohawk Park on Tulsa's
northwestern side, seldom freezes so hard it can be used for ice-skating and
iceboating, but it did this particular winter.

W. G. Skelly, founder of Skelly Oil, was a Tulsa
leader responsible for Tulsa's first airport and
numerous other civic affairs. The football stadium
at Tulsa University is named for him.

The Haynes-Patrick Auto Supply store at 201 East 2nd Street (ca. 1920).

KVOO moved to Tulsa from Bristow in 1926 in the very early days of radio. The first towers and broadcast facilities were on Reservoir Hill.

A Franklin automobile owned by the E. A. Fuller Real Estate company. From left, Nellie, Frank, and baby Frances Fuller. The woman holding the baby is unidentified (ca. 1920s).

The burned-out remains of Greenwood Avenue north of the railroad tracks, the day after the race riot in June 1921.

The interior lobby of the Ritz Theater. The beautiful movie house was the last of the leading downtown theaters to open (1926) and the first to close (1962).

Lura Lynn Douglas and Doris Clarke enjoy a Junior League "aerial tea party" in 1920. The pilot is Duncan McIntyre, pioneer operator of a Tulsa airport.

The Masonic Temple at 7th and Boston was completed in 1922, about three years before this view was recorded. The Masons used the taller portion of the building for meetings, a dining room, and offices, using the entrance on the Boston Street side. They rented the second-floor spaces to offices such as Ford Bridges Dentistry. As shown here, street-level storefronts were rented to a cleaners, an appliance store, a hat shop, a cafeteria, and Monk's Drugstore. The motorcycle parked at the corner was used for drugstore deliveries.

A parade float participates in Tulsa's first International Petroleum Exposition in 1923. The first I.P.E. was mostly confined to the street in front of the Brady Theater. The show later moved to the Tulsa Fairgrounds.

In 1922, Tulsa Printing Company occupied the street-level retail space of the Brownlee Apartment building in the 500 block of South Detroit. Apartments occupied the 2nd and 3rd floors. Fannie and Jules Mish owned the building.

Delegates to an American Legion convention in 1920. Everyone wore a hat in those days, boys included.

The Oklahoma Tire & Supply store at 2nd and Cincinnati, as the name
implies, sold tires and auto accessories in the 1920s.

Water was an insoluble problem in Tulsa until the Spavinaw Water project was completed in 1924—about the time this view was recorded at the Sand Springs Bottling Company, in the suburb of that name west of the city. Before 1924, the city drew all water from the Arkansas River, choked with the waste from up to a dozen oil refineries. The water was so bad, few people would drink it, giving rise to many water-bottling companies in and around Tulsa.

The maintenance crew of the Tulsa Street Railway company in
1920. Streetcars plied the streets of Tulsa from 1905 to 1935.

Known as the Exchange National Bank until the Great Depression, the bank doing business in this building renamed itself the National Bank of Tulsa and finally the Bank of Oklahoma. Today, the bank resides in the 50-story Williams Tower a block away. The building shown here, now called the 320 South Boston building, was expanded to its present size in 1927 and was the tallest building in Tulsa for four decades.

Tulsa Street Railway car #455 rests outside the car barn on West 5th Street in 1920.

The source of Tulsa's water supply since 1924, Spavinaw Lake. Until this lake and water system were completed, Tulsa's water was reportedly potable, but just barely. The two daily newspapers, the *World* and the *Democrat,* had different ideas about building a new supply system. The *World,* backed by the Chamber of Commerce, won, and the largest, most expensive water system in the nation, up to that time, was completed. The lake and dam are 70 miles to the northeast of Tulsa. The water flows by gravity.

Union Depot, completed in 1931 on the designs of R. C. Stephens, was a fine example of art deco architecture featuring thematic details inspired by Native American art. Closed to passenger rail service in 1967, the building's interior succumbed to looters. Today the depot stands resurrected as an office building.

The Alvin Plaza hotel in 1928 on the northeast corner of 7th and Main. The international Barbershop Harmony Society was formed on the mezzanine in 1938 by O. C. Cash and Rupert Hall. Hall was the first president of the group, and Cash called himself founder and temporary 3rd assistant vice-president.

Boston Avenue from 6th in 1927 just after the completion of the Philtower, tallest building, at center-right. Soon after this image was recorded, the National Bank of Tulsa tower would become the tallest building in the city. Residences in view mingle with office buildings. The rounded building in the foreground is a Sunoco filling station. Vandevers advertises itself as a "Store For All The People" on the building at left.

Several private business leaders guaranteed payment for construction of Tulsa's first airport in 1928-29. This building was used until a permanent terminal opened in 1932. In the spring of 1929, Tulsa's airport was the busiest in the world, thanks to oil company traffic able to afford tickets.

Charles Lindbergh landed at McIntyre Airport, at Admiral and Sheridan, on September 30, 1927. The two men outside his plane are "wing walkers," whose job was to stablize the airplane while it taxied.

The Wright Building and two-story annex at 3rd and Cheyenne in 1926.

Looking west on 4th Street from Cincinnati in the winter of 1929. The buildings on the right are the YMCA, the Kennedy office building, and the National Bank of Tulsa, tallest building in the city at that time. On the left is City Hall and the back of the Cosden building.

A streetcar turns south on Main from 5th Street. The McFarland building is on the left and the Sinclair, Vandevers, and Thompson buildings on the right (ca. 1929).

Spartan Aircraft Factory in 1929 on North Sheridan Road at Virgin, in an area known as Tulsa Heights just north of the Frisco Railroad tracks. The Tulsa Municipal Airport is just outside the photograph at upper-left. Spartan was established the year before when Skelly Oil bought out Midcontinent Aircraft. Skelly's majority owner became J. Paul Getty, who later established the Spartan Trailer manufacturing facility (for mobile homes) at this location. Getty lived in Tulsa throughout the 1930s.

Tulsa Little Theatre presents amateur productions of plays and musicals. Early on, shows were held in a tent, but the group would later have its own building on Delaware, south of 15th Street. Today various performing arts centers are used for presentations.

The Philtower under
construction, July 14, 1927.

The Philtower lobby from
the south entrance.

The view from the top of the just completed Philtower in 1927 shows the
Mayo Hotel, tall building at center, and the Arkansas River. On the west bank
of the river is the Cosden Refinery, now called the Sun Refinery.

The southwest entrance to the Coliseum, 6th and Elgin (ca. 1930).

Laying pipe for the Spavinaw Water project in May 1923.

The Mayo Hotel on the northeast corner of 5th and Cheyenne. The mix of commercial structures and residences here is visual evidence of the evolution of cities, in which business districts frequently replace the communities to which they often cater.

Charles Lindbergh visited Tulsa on September 30, 1927, a few months after his solo Atlantic flight from New York to Paris. Mayor Newblock (at center) greeted Lindbergh, left, and Lt. Goebel at McIntyre Airport. They are standing in front of the *Spirit of St. Louis,* now on display at the Smithsonian in Washington, D.C.

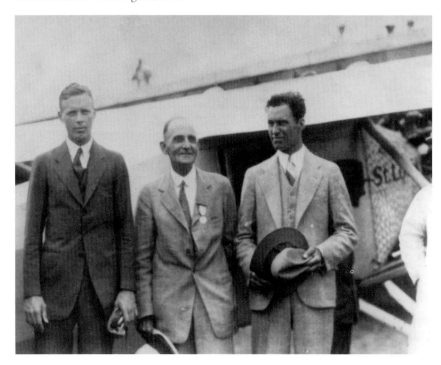

U.S. Army blimp #C-71 visits Tulsa in 1929 at hangar #3. The cars are parked on Apache Street. A few years later, Tulsa Municipal Airport was constructed, approximately where the blimp is resting. Hangar #3 is still in use today.

The Majestic movie theater in the 1930s was located at 410 South Main. This theater was one of the "big four" downtown, until they began closing in 1962. The others were the Orpheum, Rialto, and Ritz.

Red Caps at the Union Depot. As did hotel bellmen, the Red Caps (their hats were red) carried luggage to and from the trains (ca. 1930s).

The Philtower and the Philcade,
at right (ca. 1930).

The Rose Garden (lower-right) just south of Woodward Park on Peoria. The Arkansas River and 21st Street bridge are visible in the upper-left. The mansion at lower-left is now the home of the Tulsa Historical Society.

A Phillips 66 Petroleum full-service station at 15th and Cincinnati advertises Benzo-Gas. It "does what gasoline can't—the real motor fuel" (ca. 1930). Phillips has since merged with Conoco.

St. Paul's Methodist Church was located in the 1930s at 15th and Quaker and is still active at that location today. Claude P. Zenor was the minister. The smaller sign leaning on the other is advertising a Friday evening ice cream social. This church was begun by Sylvester Morris, a traveling preacher credited with starting more than 15 churches, many in Tulsa.

Pierce Pennant motel, restaurant, and gasoline station, several miles east of Tulsa at 12100 East 11 Street on Highway 66, was first-class in 1930. The city limits extend well beyond this point today.

The lobby of the Alvin Plaza Hotel at 7th and Main (ca. 1930s).

Skelly Stadium, in view here on a football game day in the early 1930s, seated around 15,000. The University of Tulsa is visible at top-right. On 11th Street, two blocks west of Harvard, the stadium has been expanded several times and is still home to the Tulsa University Golden Hurricane.

A 1930s Peoples Ice Company delivery truck. The lettering on the truck advertises a five-digit telephone number: 2-8144.

"Two Oklahoma Injuns" reads the description: Patrick Hurley, left, and Will Rogers. Hurley was U.S. Secretary of War from 1929 to 1933 and served as an Army general during World War II, among other roles. Rogers was born in 1879 in the Indian Territory, rising to national fame as a much-loved humorist and pundit. Among his timeless quips was, "Be thankful we are not getting all the government we are paying for." "I never met a man I didn't like," he said.

Oil tycoon Waite Phillips, brother to Frank Phillips of Phillips 66, lived in this mansion from 1929 to 1938, when he moved from Tulsa. He gave the property to the citizens of Tulsa, stipulating that it must be used as an art museum. It is reported that Phillips never liked living in this house.

Headquarters for Oklahoma Natural Gas, at the northwest corner of 7th and Boston, until their move into a new building. This structure is one of many in Tulsa on the National Historic Register. Behind it is the Alvin Plaza Hotel, where the Barbershop Harmony Society was formed in 1938 (ca. 1930s).

The Skelly mansion on the southeast corner of 21st and Madison still maintains its eloquence. Oilman W. G. Skelly lived here until his death. It has since been extensively remodeled by subsequent owners.

The Tulsa police station in the 1930s at 4th and Elgin. The building was razed when the police moved into a new building in the civic center next to the county courthouse.

The K. C. Auto Hotel in 1935. The parking garage remained in use until 2006. Aside from parking, auto service, and lunch, one could also rent one of these new Fords. Parking was 35 cents for four hours or 50 cents for 12 hours.

Tulsa was a busy place when this 1930s aerial was recorded, facing north-northeast.

North on Lewis Avenue at 4th Place (ca. 1930).

The Tulsa Police reserve officers (October 1934).

George "Machine Gun" Kelly in handcuffs after he was arrested on September 25, 1933, in Memphis, Tennessee. He is escorted by Stanley Rogers, Oklahoma County sheriff (left), H. E. Anderson, special agent of the U.S. Department of Justice (holding chain, at center), and W. C. "Rube" Gears, U.S. Marshal in Oklahoma City. Kelly lived and worked in Tulsa for five years as a runner for the city's leading bootleggers before running off with his boss's wife. He and several others kidnapped Charles F. Urschel, an Oklahoma City millionaire in July 1933. After his arrest, he was convicted 18 days later. He died in prison of a heart attack on July 18, 1954, his 59th birthday.

The Coliseum played host to many memorable events from the day it opened until it burned down in the fall of 1952. The first event in the arena was an ice hockey game on January 1, 1929. Shown here is a playoff game on March 22, 1935, with Tulsa beating Kansas City 5 to 1.

North on Main from 4th about 1937. Buses have replaced streetcar service, discontinued only two years earlier and the tracks removed.

Vandevers department store was originally located on the alley, halfway between Main and Boston on 5th Street. The store later expanded into the building on the left and another building that opened onto Main Street attached by a bridge across the alley. Like all other downtown department stores, Vandevers eventually closed and moved to suburban shopping centers. The two cars in front of the store are Chevrolets.

One of several large ice companies in Tulsa in 1935, the Tulsa Ice Company was on the southeast corner of 6th and Xanthus. The delivery truck is a 1935 Ford. At that time, ice was delivered door to door, the same as milk.

The Hunt building at 4th and Main was home to the Brown-Dunkin department store for decades. To the right of the Hunt building is the Haber building, with a Rexall Drug store. Next door is Seidenbach's, an upscale women's clothing store. To the left is Tulsa Savings and Loan, the Orpheum Theater, and the Pioneer (Southwestern Bell) Telephone building and the Cosden Building (ca. 1934).

Aviation has been of key importance to Tulsa since the first airport terminal was built in 1928. This is hangar #3 in the early 1930s. The crew is doing maintenance on a Fokker Trimotor airplane.

Will Rogers High School, 3509 East 5th Place, opened its doors to the first class in
September 1939, just a few years before this photograph was made. Built as a WPA
project, it is still one of the city's most beautiful schools.

# THE OIL CAPITAL OF THE WORLD

## (1940–1972)

Tulsa expanded its aviation industry in 1942 during World War II with the construction and operation of the Douglas Bomber plant, a mile-long building adjacent the airport. The plant built A-26 and B-24 bombers. Immediately following the war, American Airlines put its main maintenance facility in the same area. Tulsa returned to being the Oil Capital of the World for the next three decades, until the title was relinquished to Houston as oil moved offshore and to foreign fields.

Television came to the city on November 30, 1949, when KOTV, Channel 6, began broadcasting. The first large downtown building since 1932, the 1st National Bank, was built and occupied in 1950. The first suburban shopping center, Utica Square, opened in 1952. The four-lane Turner Turnpike to Oklahoma City opened at the same time with the promise to voters that it would be a free road in only 15 years. More than 5 decades later, a toll is still charged.

Pennington's and Norman Angel's drive-ins opened in the early 1950s with the onset of the drive-in restaurant craze. The popular Harden's Hamburgers added Kentucky Fried Chicken to its menu when KFC was an unknown franchise. The new county courthouse opened in 1957. The old site is now a 32-story office building. Sears moved away from downtown in 1958, relocating its store on the eastern edge of the city at 21st and Yale. Today, that area is considered midtown.

Despite the repeal of Prohibition in 1933, Oklahoma remained a dry state until August 1, 1959. Until 1959, bootleggers would deliver whiskey to one's home for $5 a bottle. Package liquor stores opened and with the slow change of regulations, open bars are now legal in Tulsa and most counties of the state.

Tulsa had three all-white high schools and one all-black from 1940 to 1955. Edison High School opened in 1955 with the first graduating class in 1958. The schools began integration that year.

After World War II, Tulsa became noted for television and radio evangelists like Oral Roberts. Roberts opened Oral Roberts University in 1962.

The Arkansas River was completely tamed with the completion of the Keystone Dam northwest of Tulsa in 1964. The river is now tightly controlled, for barge traffic to and from the Tulsa Port at Catoosa.

A school debate at Central High School (ca. 1940).

South on Cincinnati from the railroad viaduct ca. 1940. The large, dark brick building in the center is the Hotel Tulsa. L. C. Clark, of the Clark-Darland Hardware company at right, was mayor of Tulsa in the mid-1950s and was the man responsible for initiating the city's first expressway.

The west side of Main at 3rd Street about 1940. J. C. Penney later moved to a new building half a block south. Kress, a large national chain, had entrances on Main and around the corner on 3rd Street. The Main Street theater is just north of Penney's and, not shown in this image, the Tulsa Theater is directly across the street.

Frank's Pig Stand between 14th and 15th streets on Boston ca. 1940. It was one of several drive-ins popular among high school students.

Crockett's Drug and Ward Chemical are open for business on the northwest corner of 10th and Main in 1941. The site is now a parking lot for Tulsa Community College, across the street to the east in the old Sinclair Oil building.

The heart of Tulsa's shopping district was 4th to 6th on Main Street when this view was made in the early 1940s. Few of these businesses are still running today and those that are have different names. Skaggs moved from this location into the old Sears downtown building about 1958-59 and later to other locations. After a series of name changes, it is now Albertson's. Sears had moved to 21st and Yale in 1958, then considered the eastern edge of Tulsa.

One of the numerous A-26 bombers manufactured in Tulsa during World War II. Many women had jobs building the bombers.

A dedication ceremony inside Air Force Building #3, also called the Douglas Bomber plant. The plane is a B-24 Liberator. The federal government later deeded the mile-long building to the City of Tulsa.

World War II war bonds and stamps were sold at booths like this one in all large cities. This booth, in front of the 1st National Bank at 4th and Main, was operated by the American Legion and their auxiliary. When $18 worth of stamps were collected, one would receive a $25 bond.

The *Tulsamerican* B-24 bomber in 1944, manufactured at the Douglas plant for overseas service in World War II.

Now lovingly nicknamed "Old Lady Brady," this auditorium opened in 1915 at 105 West Brady. A new entrance was added following World War II and the building was called the Tulsa Municipal Theater. It seats about 2,500.

A Tulsa mansion, at 405 East 19 Street. It is one of many similar houses in that district.

Employees of the Adams Ford Motor Company at 5th and Detroit about 1946. Neither the building nor the company exists today.

Looking south on Cincinnati from 18th about 1946. The buildings that housed the Phillips 66 station were still standing in 2007.

The "center of Tulsa" for more than two decades following World War II was 4th and Main. This 1947-48 view shows Brown-Dunkin department store, at left, the Ritz movie theater, at right, and Crown Drugs, at center. None of these buildings exists today.

Country and Western legend Bob Wills and his Texas Playboys at Cain's Ballroom during a KVOO radio broadcast (late 1940s).

A group of students at Lanier Elementary School in 1948. Lanier
is at 17th and Harvard.

An American Legion vehicle participates in a parade in 1949. The Santa Fe railroad sign is on the Atlas Life building between 4th and 5th on Boston. At this time, travel by rail had entered the beginning of its end. Tulsa has been without passenger rail service for more than three decades.

The Elks Lodge, before the group moved to the suburbs in the 1960s.

Auto racing was a main event at the Tulsa Fairgrounds. Here driver Al Lemons shows off his car #19.

The Budweiser Clydesdales were in town for a parade ca. 1950. Here they have pulled to a stop between 10th and 11th where Main Street straightens into a true north-south direction.

Looking east on 3rd Street from Main ca. 1950. The Hotel Tulsa is at center-left.
Pedestrians are passing Zales, according to the clock, about one-thirty in the afternoon.

Facing north on Boston from 8th Street in 1952. The scaffolding at center-left is for the construction of the Chamber of Commerce building at 616 South Boston. The chamber used the building for 50 years before moving to the Williams Center tower.

Telephones in automobiles were very unusual half a century ago. Sitting in a 1952
Studebaker, this Southwestern Bell employee demonstrates the radio telephone.

Boy Scout Troop #1. The troop was organized by the Presbyterian Church of Tulsa in 1910.

In view from the air is the University of Tulsa campus ca. 1950. The school's library sits at the head of the oval. Kendall Hall is just to the right and above the library. Skelly Stadium is in the upper right. The private university was Kendall College when it moved to Tulsa in 1908 from Muskogee, Oklahoma.

The Sun Oil Company building, formerly Sunray-DX, is under construction in 1953 at the corner of 9th and Detroit.

First Street between Cheyenne and Frankford was Tulsa's red-light district
for decades, beginning with the oil boom days. One of the most infamous
"sporting clubs" was the May Rooms, on the second floor above the shops
at left. What is peculiar about this image is that the Ford car in the center of
the street clearly has no driver.

Glenn Dobbs, head football coach and athletic director at Tulsa University, shows off a trophy to a recruit. Dobbs played at Tulsa from 1943 to 1945 and later in the Canadian Football League. He became athletic director in 1958 and named himself head football coach in early 1960. He was a driving force to enlarge Skelly Stadium to hold more than 40,000 fans.

Harry's Cafe occupied this location at 1st and Boulder ca. 1950s. George and John Bullette, Delaware Indians, once operated a general store at this spot, bringing in goods by mule and ox wagon before rail service was established. The historical marker at right identifies their store as the first in Tulsa.

This was the corner of 4th and Boston about 1954, featuring the building known as the Cosden.

The Philcade Building at 5th
and Boston was one of the Waite
Phillips buildings (ca. 1955).

164

A publicity photo for the Hopalong Cassidy Savings Club. William Boyd, who played Cassidy, is pictured on the cardboard cutout behind the girls (ca. 1955).

Shown here is the Spartan Manufacturing plant near the airport
on north Sheridan Road.

One of several Tulsa neighborhood movie theaters, the Delman at 15th and Lewis is showing Claudette Colbert's 1949 film *Bride for Sale*. Crown Drugs is on the corner, as they were at many main intersections.

These women turn out at 4th and Main in the summer of 1955 for a
"Tulsa Beautiful Campaign." The drive was to clean, fix, and paint houses
and businesses—and keep the streets swept.

Receiving a bouquet of roses, Anita Bryant, a graduate of Will Rogers High School in 1958, was 1st Runner-up to Miss America. She would become a well-known recording star.

Veterans Day parades have always been popular in Tulsa. This mid-1950s parade shows six World War veterans following Dode McIntosh, a World War I veteran and the last appointed chief of the Creeks. The chief is elected today.

Looking northeast at Admiral Place and Sheridan Road during the winter months. McCormick Machinery was the Caterpillar dealer at that time (ca. 1955).

In 1957, Walgreens occupied the northeast corner of 4th and Main. The building was originally the home of the 1st National Bank before the bank moved to its present location at 5th and Boston. Opened in 1950, the new bank building was the first major high-rise building constructed in downtown Tulsa since before the Depression and World War II.

This Kress store was laid out in an "L" shape with entrances on 3rd Street and Main Street. Kress was a chain of dimestores, frequently housed in architecturally interesting buildings, that carried inexpensive brands.

A poster in the Chamber of Commerce window promotes the opening of the 1954 Tulsa Oilers season. Grayle Howlett, at far-right, was the club owner. The team is now called the Tulsa Drillers and is owned by Chuck Lamson.

The Pythian building at 5th and Boulder. The Western Union office, housed in this building, is shown here at far-right.

The west side of Main Street between 3rd and 4th showing, from left, Palace Clothiers, Woolworth's, Froug's clothing store, and the Alexander building, formerly the Robinson Hotel. The Alexander building was later leveled to allow for a new J. C. Penney store and more recently for an expansion of the Tulsa World newspaper, which now owns the entire city block.

Bordens Cafe occupied a small building near the northwest corner of 6th and Boston. It was demolished to make room for today's Enterprise office building. Borden's had numerous cafes and cafeterias throughout Tulsa for many years.

The 1957 flood creeps up the levy protecting the Public Service Company's Tulsa power plant on the west side of the Arkansas River at about 31st Street.

Flooding of the Arkansas River was long a problem in Tulsa, especially after the suburbs extended south along the river. Here the river is out of its banks again in 1957, as volunteers turn out in large numbers to fill and place sandbangs to contain the rising water along Riverside Drive. The problem was finally solved with the completion of the Keystone Dam 18 miles upstream.

This new 1957 Plymouth was buried on the west side of Denver between 5th and 6th streets immediately adjacent the Tulsa County Courthouse. This couple is looking at the car parked at 4th and Main prior to its burial in the concrete vault. The vault will be opened as part of the state's centennial celebration in 2007.

Sleek against a curtain of cumulus clouds, an American Airlines DC-6 awaits its next takeoff at Tulsa Municipal Airport. American has been an important employer in Tulsa since World War II. The art deco terminal building opened in 1932 and closed in 1961, the year today's airport was completed.

Looking north on Main Street during a fire prevention parade ca. 1958. The major department stores shown include Brown-Dunkin (at center), Vandevers (far right), Streets (at left, in the Mayo building), and Clarkes (just beyond the Brown-Dunkin sign).

Tulsa was a busy retail area when this photo was made in the late 1950s. The National Bank of Tulsa, the 1st National Bank, and Philtower buildings dominate the night skyline. Facing northeast from 6th and Main, popular locations included Vandevers and Brown Dunkin department stores, Clarkes and Streets clothing store, Skaggs Drug (foreground), Jenkins Music, Bishop's Restaurant, and Peacock and Boswell's Jewelry. Boswell was a fixture on Main Street since the early 1900s.

This aerial view shows the general area of 1st and Kenosha. It is at this point that 1st Street and all other downtown streets bend to a true east-west direction. Downtown Tulsa's streets are approximately 30 degrees off true east-west as a result of being built parallel to the railroad tracks in 1882.

A livestock auction at the Tulsa State Fair (ca. 1950s).

Pennington's Drive-in on south Peoria was a popular eating establishment for decades, especially among teenagers.

Sunray-DX celebrates its 50th anniversary ca. 1964. Governor Henry Bellmon stands at center with his arm in a sling.

Governor J. Howard Edmondson speaks at the dedication of the Broken
Arrow Expressway (ca. 1960).

Converging at 31st and Yale were two main streets and the Broken Arrow Expressway. When all the street construction was complete, a dedication was needed. Tulsa mayor Jim Maxwell sits to the left of the podium at the dedication (early 1960s).

Boswell's Jewelry was a key tenant on Main Street in several locations. This is the interior of Boswell's during a grand opening (ca. 1960).

Dode McIntosh, chief of the Creek Indians, in his full regalia (ca. 1960).

The south side of 5th Street at Boulder in 1965. The Stansberry building houses the Brown Boot Shop, Montague Fabrics, a book and magazine store, Markie's Grill, and Marilou's Pastry Shop. Skaggs Drug occupies the old Sears building across Boulder. The very attractive Skaggs building was built for Sears at the end of the art deco construction period in the early 1930s. It was demolished to make room for the Oneok (Oklahoma Natural Gas) building.

The Olympic Apartments near Riverside Drive were new in the 1960s. The spire at top-left belongs to Holy Family Catholic Church. The dark, tallest building is the American Airlines building, now a parking lot.

A group of Will Rogers Rotary Club members visit with
Oklahoma governor (later U.S. senator) Henry Bellman, third
from left on the sofa (ca. 1960s).

A home show in the Civic Center arena (ca. 1965).

A bird's-eye view of Boston Avenue Methodist Church at
13th and Boston.

Tulsa Fairgrounds between Louisville and Yale from 15th to 21st streets. The large building is the Expo Center, originally called the IPE building (February 1966).

Will Rogers High School in August 1965. The school opened in September 1939 and has been expanded several times since. When the school was completed, none of the houses shown in this view existed.

The Tulsa skyline during the construction of the inter-dispersal loop that connects six expressways (ca. 1970).

# Notes on the Photographs

These notes, listed by page number, attempt to include all aspects known of the photographs. Each of the photographs is identified by the page number, photograph's title or description, photographer and collection, archive, and call or box number when applicable. Although every attempt was made to collect all available data, in some cases complete data was unavailable due to the age and condition of some of the photographs and records.

**II**  **SKYLINE**
Jerry L. Cornelius Collection
XA062 Skyline

**VI**  **GOLDEN DRILLER**
Jerry L. Cornelius Collection
XA213 Golden Driller

**X**  **CYCLISTS**
The Beryl Ford Collection
A0991 Valley Water Mills

**2**  **TULSA BAND**
The Beryl Ford Collection
A1142 Tulsas first band

**3**  **MISSION STUDENTS**
The Beryl Ford Collection
A1152 Presbyterian Mission

**4**  **FRISCO RAILROAD BRIDGE**
The Beryl Ford Collection
A1205 Frisco RR Bridge

**5**  **DOWNTOWN**
The Beryl Ford Collection
A0083 2nd & Main

**6**  **SMALL RESIDENCE**
The Beryl Ford Collection
A1239 202 S Maybelle

**7**  **CATTLE**
The Beryl Ford Collection
A0164 Cattle Drive

**8**  **STANDPIPE HILL**
The Beryl Ford Collection
A1274 Tulsa 1892

**9**  **GENERAL STORE**
The Beryl Ford Collection
A1243 Archer Store 1893

**10**  **MAIN STREET**
The Beryl Ford Collection
A0159 2nd & Main

**11**  **FIRST POST OFFICE**
The Beryl Ford Collection
A0165 Tulsa's first p. o.

**12**  **GENERAL MERCHANT**
The Beryl Ford Collection
A0168 JM Hall Store 1894

**13**  **T.J. ARCHER STORE**
The Beryl Ford Collection
A0152 TJ Archers store

**14**  **COLONEL CALKINS**
The Beryl Ford Collection
A0089 Col. Edward Calkins

**15**  **PALACE MARKET**
The Beryl Ford Collection
A0796 Palace Market

**16**  **RIVER CROSSING**
The Beryl Ford Collection
A0167 River Ferry

**17**  **EAST MAIN STREET**
The Beryl Ford Collection
A0156 East Side of Main

**18**  **LIVERY BARN**
The Beryl Ford Collection
A0171 Livery Barn

**19**  **MISSION SCHOOL**
The Beryl Ford Collection
A0151 Presbyterian Mission

**20**  **PADDLE WHEEL FERRY**
The Beryl Ford Collection
A0091 Ferry on Ark. River

**21**  **MAIN STREET FIRE**
The Beryl Ford Collection
A0090 Business Dist. fire

**22**  **FIRST TELEPHONE BOARD**
The Beryl Ford Collection
A1016 Robert Hall

**23**  **TULSA HOSPITAL**
The Beryl Ford Collection
A0099 Tulsa Hospital

**24**  **LILAH LINDSEY**
The Beryl Ford Collection
A0711 Lilah Lindsey

**25**  **BUFFALO BILL**
The Beryl Ford Collection
A0378 Pawnee & Buffalo Bill

**26**  **FRISCO RR DEPOT**
The Beryl Ford Collection
A0174 Crowd at Frisco Rail

**27**  **ALCORN HOTEL**
The Beryl Ford Collection
A0790 Alcorn Hotel Lobby

**28**  **SUE BLAND #1**
The Beryl Ford Collection
A0100 Sue Bland No. 1

**29**  **TULSA RESIDENCE**
The Beryl Ford Collection
A0728 Residence on 6th

**30**  **SKYLINE VIEW**
The Beryl Ford Collection
A0802 Skyline 1903

**31 TULSA BANKING COMPANY**
The Beryl Ford Collection
A0714 Tulsa Banking

**32 WOODWARD PARK**
The Beryl Ford Collection
A0638 Woodward Park

**34 GLENN POOL**
The Beryl Ford Collection
A0299 Glen Pool Oil Field

**35 SOUTH LANSING**
The Beryl Ford Collection
A0786 402 S Lansing

**36 STREET-PAVING TEAMS**
The Beryl Ford Collection
A1238 2nd and Maybelle

**37 PROMOTIONAL BAND**
The Beryl Ford Collection
A2003 Tulsa Band, Washington

**38 FRISCO RAILROAD DEPOT**
The Beryl Ford Collection
A0983 Frisco Depot

**39 ARCHER RESIDENCE**
The Beryl Ford Collection
A1246 Archer Home 1906

**40 FIRST FOOT BRIDGE**
The Beryl Ford Collection
A0017 Ark. River Bridge

**41 BRADY HOTEL**
The Beryl Ford Collection
A0300 Brady Hotel

**42 MAIN STREET**
The Beryl Ford Collection
A0007 Main Street ca. 1909

**43 WCTU**
The Beryl Ford Collection
A0818 Womens Temperance

**44 STREETCAR RAILS**
The Beryl Ford Collection
A4030 Main St South

**45 HOTEL TULSA**
The Beryl Ford Collection
A1109 Hotel Tulsa 1923

**46 TULSA'S FINEST**
The Beryl Ford Collection
A0109 Tulsa Police 1910

**47 SHACKLE'S DRUGSTORE**
The Beryl Ford Collection
A0108 Shackle's Drug Store

**48 FAMILY OUTING**
The Beryl Ford Collection
A0029-A Family outing

**49 MODERN PRINT SHOP**
The Beryl Ford Collection
A0726 Print Shop

**50 BOY SCOUT TROOP**
The Beryl Ford Collection
A0722 Boy Scout Troop

**51 FIRE WAGON**
The Beryl Ford Collection
A0301 Tulsa Fire Dept

**52 FIRST FOOT BRIDGE**
The Beryl Ford Collection
A1989 Fike & Dischler

**53 EAST END CAFE**
The Beryl Ford Collection
A0735 East End Cafe

**54 PROMOTING TULSA**
The Beryl Ford Collection
A0744 Tulsa Band

**55 BARBERSHOP**
The Beryl Ford Collection
A1086 barbers

**56 TULSA HIGH SCHOOL**
The Beryl Ford Collection
A4031 Tulsa High - 1915

**57 THIRD STREET**
The Beryl Ford Collection
A0302 East on 3rd

**58 YMCA**
The Beryl Ford Collection
A0124 YMCA Bldg

**59 YOUNG ADULTS**
The Beryl Ford Collection
A1134 Arkansas River Picnic

**60 WAR PARADE**
The Beryl Ford Collection
A0078 WWI Main St Parade

**61 AMBULANCE COMPANY**
The Beryl Ford Collection
A1153 Tulsa Ambulance Co.

**62 WEST TULSA FLOOD**
The Beryl Ford Collection
A0030-A West Tulsa

**65 TULSA LIBRARY**
The Beryl Ford Collection
A0783 Carnagie Library

**66 STREET FLOOD**
The Beryl Ford Collection
A1214 Flood

**67 AMY COMSTOCK**
The Beryl Ford Collection
A1577 Amy Comstock

**68 LAKE YAHOLA**
The Beryl Ford Collection
A0210 Ice Skating & Sailing

**69 W.G. SKELLY**
The Beryl Ford Collection
A0625 WG Skelly

**70 AUTO SUPPLY STORE**
The Beryl Ford Collection
A0723 Haynes-Patrick Auto

**71 KVOO**
The Beryl Ford Collection
A0719 KVOO

**72 FRANKLIN AUTOMOBILE**
The Beryl Ford Collection
A0030-B Fuller family

**73 1921 RACE RIOT**
The Beryl Ford Collection
A2416 Tulsa Race Riot

**74 RITZ THEATRE INTERIOR**
Jerry L. Cornelius Collection
XA498 Ritz Theater Lobby

**75 AERIAL TEA PARTY**
The Beryl Ford Collection
A0284 Duncan McIntyre

**76 MASONIC TEMPLE**
The Beryl Ford Collection
A1607 Masonic Bldg

**77 PARADE FLOAT**
The Beryl Ford Collection
A1479 IPE Parade Float

**78 TULSA PRINTING COMPANY**
The Beryl Ford Collection
A0574 Tulsa Printing Co.

**79 AMERICAN LEGION**
The Beryl Ford Collection
A1657 American Legion

**80 TIRE & SUPPLY**
The Beryl Ford Collection
A1606 OTASCO 2nd & Elgin

**81 SAND SPRINGS BOTTLING**
The Beryl Ford Collection
A1180 Sand Springs Bottling

**82 STREET RAILWAY COMPANY**
The Beryl Ford Collection
A1490 Tulsa Street Railway

**83 NBT BUILDING**
The Beryl Ford Collection
A0550 NBT Building

**84 CAR #455**
The Beryl Ford Collection
A1488 Tulsa Street Railway

**85 SPAVINAW LAKE**
The Beryl Ford Collection
A0180 Spavinaw Lake & Dam

**86 UNION DEPOT**
The Beryl Ford Collection
A0528 Union Station

**87 ALVIN PLAZA HOTEL**
The Beryl Ford Collection
A1287 Alvin Hotel

**88 BOSTON AVENUE**
The Beryl Ford Collection
A1321 Tulsa Skyline 1928

**89 FIRST AIRPORT**
The Beryl Ford Collection
A0044 Tulsa Mun. Airport

**90 LINDBERGH LANDS**
The Beryl Ford Collection
A0120 Spirit of St. Louis

**91 WRIGHT BUILDING**
The Beryl Ford Collection
A0544 Wright Building

**92 4TH STREET**
The Beryl Ford Collection
A1601 Downtown in Winter

**93 MAIN STREET**
The Beryl Ford Collection
A1609 5th From Main

**94 SPARTAN AIRCRAFT**
The Beryl Ford Collection
A0057 Spartan Aircraft

**95 TULSA LITTLE THEATRE**
The Beryl Ford Collection
A0755 Tulsa Little Theatre

**96 PHILTOWER**
The Beryl Ford Collection
A1104 Philtower Construction

**97 PHILTOWER LOBBY**
The Beryl Ford Collection
A0859 Philtower Lobby

**98 MAYO HOTEL**
The Beryl Ford Collection
A1573 River from Philtower

**99 COLISEUM**
The Beryl Ford Collection
A1151 Coliseum

**100 LAYING PIPE**
The Beryl Ford Collection
A1121 Pipe at Spavinaw

**101 MAYO HOTEL**
The Beryl Ford Collection
A1111 Mayo Hotel 1925

**102 CHARLES LINDBERGH**
The Beryl Ford Collection
A0045 McIntyre Airport

**103 BLIMP #C-71**
The Beryl Ford Collection
A0043 U.S. Army Blimp C-71

**104 THE MAJESTIC**
The Beryl Ford Collection
A0115 Majestic Theater

**105 RED CAPS**
The Beryl Ford Collection
A0827 Red Caps

**106 PHILTOWER**
The Beryl Ford Collection
A0858 Philtower

**107 ROSE GARDEN**
The Beryl Ford Collection
A0525 Rose Garden

**108 PHILLIPS 66 STATION**
The Beryl Ford Collection
A0518 15th & Cincinnati

**109 ST. PAUL'S METHODIST**
The Beryl Ford Collection
A1704 St Pauls Methodist

**110 PIERCE PENNANT MOTEL**
The Beryl Ford Collection
A0734 Pierce Penant Motel

**111 ALVIN PLAZA HOTEL**
The Beryl Ford Collection
A0808 Alvin Hotel Lobby

**112 SKELLY STADIUM**
The Beryl Ford Collection
A0178 Game Day at Skelly

**113 PEOPLES ICE COMPANY**
The Beryl Ford Collection
A0263 Peoples Ice Co

**114 "TWO OKLAHOMA INJUNS"**
The Beryl Ford Collection
A0056 W. Rogers & P. Hurley

**115 PHILLIPS HOME**
The Beryl Ford Collection
A0561 Philbrook

**116 NATURAL GAS BUILDING**
The Beryl Ford Collection
A1719 ONG Bldg

**117 SKELLY MANSION**
The Beryl Ford Collection
A0560 Skelly Mansion

**118 TULSA POLICE STATION**
The Beryl Ford Collection
A0476 Police Station

**119 K.C. AUTO HOTEL**
The Beryl Ford Collection
A0118 KC Auto Hotel

**120 TULSA IN 1930**
The Beryl Ford Collection
A1920 Aerial from the West

**121 LEWIS AVENUE**
The Beryl Ford Collection
A0720 Lewis & 4th Pl

**122 POLICE RESERVE**
The Beryl Ford Collection
A0820 Police Reserves

**123 "MACHINE GUN" KELLY**
The Beryl Ford Collection
A0435 Machine Gun Kelly

**124 COLISEUM HOCKEY**
The Beryl Ford Collection
A1267 Hockey Playoff

**125 NORTH ON MAIN STREET**
The Beryl Ford Collection
A1318 4th & Main

**126 VANDEVER'S STORE**
The Beryl Ford Collection
A0274 Vandevers

**127 TULSA ICE COMPANY**
The Beryl Ford Collection
A0248 Tulsa Ice Co

**128 HUNT BUILDING**
The Beryl Ford Collection
A1602 Hunt Bldg

**129 HANGAR #3**
The Beryl Ford Collection
A0282 Fokker Trimotor

**130** WILL ROGERS HIGH SCHOOL
The Beryl Ford Collection
A0161 Will Rogers HS

**132** SCHOOL DEBATE
The Beryl Ford Collection
A0693 School Debate

**133** SOUTH ON CINCINNATI
The Beryl Ford Collection
A0011 Cincinnati to South

**134** MAIN STREET AT 3RD
The Beryl Ford Collection
A1482 Main from 3rd 1940s

**135** FRANK'S PIG STAND
The Beryl Ford Collection
A0539 Franks Pig Stand

**136** CROCKETT'S DRUG STORE
The Beryl Ford Collection
A1722 Rexall Drugs 10th

**137** SHOPPING DISTRICT
The Beryl Ford Collection
A1599 Brown Dunkin

**138** A-26 BOMBERS
The Beryl Ford Collection
A0187 A-26 Bomber

**139** AIR FORCE BUILDING #3
The Beryl Ford Collection
A0182 Dedication Ceremony

**140** WAR BONDS BOOTH
The Beryl Ford Collection
A0281 War Stamp Booth

**141** TULSAMERICAN
The Beryl Ford Collection
A0195 Tulsamerican B-24

**142** "OLD LADY BRADY"
The Beryl Ford Collection
A1092 Brady Theater

**143** TULSA MANSION
The Beryl Ford Collection
A0784 405 E 19th

**144** ADAMS MOTOR COMPANY
The Beryl Ford Collection
A1249 Ford Agency

**145** CINCINNATI AT 18TH ST.
The Beryl Ford Collection
A0147 18th & Cinn.

**146** "CENTER OF TULSA"
The Beryl Ford Collection
A1483 Crown Drug Store

**147** BOB WILLS
The Beryl Ford Collection
A0242 Bob Wills

**148** LANIER ELEMENTARY
The Beryl Ford Collection
A1538 Lanier Auditorium

**149** AMERICAN LEGION PARADE
The Beryl Ford Collection
A1471 American Legion Parade

**150** ELKS LODGE
The Beryl Ford Collection
A0577 Elks Lodge

**151** AL LEMONS
The Beryl Ford Collection
A0506 Al Lemons

**152** BUDWEISER HORSES
The Beryl Ford Collection
A0037 1100 Block S Main

**154** HOTEL TULSA
The Beryl Ford Collection
A0122 3rd & Main

**155** BOSTON AND 8TH STREET
The Beryl Ford Collection
A0039 8th & Boston

**156** RADIO TELEPHONE
The Beryl Ford Collection
A0295 SWB Car with Phone

**157** BOY SCOUT TROOP
The Beryl Ford Collection
A1117 Boy Scout Troop #1

**158** UNIVERSITY OF TULSA
The Beryl Ford Collection
A0086 T.U. campus, 1949

**159** SUN OIL COMPANY
The Beryl Ford Collection
A0530 10th & Detroit

**160** RED LIGHT DISTRICT
The Beryl Ford Collection
A0481 May Rooms

**161** GLENN DOBBS
The Beryl Ford Collection
A0480 Glen Dobbs

**162** HARRY'S CAFE
The Beryl Ford Collection
A0521 Harry's Cafe

**163** COSDEN BUILDING
The Beryl Ford Collection
A0614 Mid Continent Bldg

**164** PHILCADE BUILDING
The Beryl Ford Collection
A0513 5th & Boston

**165** HOPALONG PROMOTION
The Beryl Ford Collection
A0488 Savings Club

**166** SPARTAN MANUFACTURING
The Beryl Ford Collection
A0533 Back of Spartan

**167** DELMAN THEATER
The Beryl Ford Collection
A0526 Delman Theater

**168** TULSA BEAUTIFUL CAMPAIGN
The Beryl Ford Collection
A0073 Tulsa Beautiful

**169** ANITA BRYANT
The Beryl Ford Collection
A0677 Anita Bryant

**170** VETERANS DAY
The Beryl Ford Collection
A0814 Veterans Day Parade

**171** ADMIRAL PLACE
The Beryl Ford Collection
A0181 Admiral Pl.

**172** WALGREENS
The Beryl Ford Collection
A1473 4th & Main

**173** KRESS STORE
The Beryl Ford Collection
A0587 Inside Store

**174** BASEBALL POSTER
The Beryl Ford Collection
A0568 Tulsa Oilers Poster

**175** PYTHIAN BUILDING
The Beryl Ford Collection
A0546 Pythian Building

**176** MAIN STREET
The Beryl Ford Collection
A0160 West side of Main

**177** BORDEN'S CAFE
The Beryl Ford Collection
A0022 Borden's Cafe 6th

**178** LEVY AT POWER PLANT
The Beryl Ford Collection
A0904 Arkansas River

**179** COMMUNITY EFFORT
The Beryl Ford Collection
A1198 1957 Flood Sandbag

**180  1957 PLYMOUTH**
The Beryl Ford Collection
A1472 Plymouth Before Burial

**181  DC-6**
The Beryl Ford Collection
A0189 American Airlines 72

**182  FIRE PREVENTION PARADE**
The Beryl Ford Collection
A1486 Street Scene

**183  NIGHT SCENE**
The Beryl Ford Collection
A1902 Night View

**184  1ST AND KENOSHA**
The Beryl Ford Collection
A1804 Aerial View

**185  LIVESTOCK AUCTION**
The Beryl Ford Collection
A0988 Tulsa State Fair

**186  PENNINGTON'S DRIVE-IN**
The Beryl Ford Collection
A0756 Drive In

**187  50TH ANNIVERSARY**
The Beryl Ford Collection
A0753 DX 50th Anniversary

**188  GOVERNOR EDMONSON**
The Beryl Ford Collection
A0750 BA Expressway Ground

**189  EXPRESSWAY DEDICATION**
The Beryl Ford Collection
A0660 31st & Yale Dedication

**190  BOSWELL'S JEWELRY**
The Beryl Ford Collection
A0563 Boswells opening

**191  DODE MCINTOSH**
The Beryl Ford Collection
A0542 Dode McIntosh

**192  STANSBERRY BUILDING**
The Beryl Ford Collection
A0035 5th & Boulder

**193  OLYMPIC APARTMENTS**
The Beryl Ford Collection
A1977 Olympia Apt Aerial 6

**194  WILL ROGERS ROTARY CLUB**
The Beryl Ford Collection
A0558 Will Rogers Rotary

**195  CIVIC CENTER**
The Beryl Ford Collection
A0644 Home Builders Show

**196  BOSTON AVENUE METHODIST**
Jerry L. Cornelius Collection
XA066 Boston Av Methodist

**197  TULSA FAIRGROUNDS**
Jerry L. Cornelius Collection
XA075 Fairgrounds, 2E92-5

**198  WILL ROGERS HIGH SCHOOL**
Jerry L. Cornelius Collection
XA184 Will Rogers HS 8D49-

**199  TULSA SKYLINE**
The Beryl Ford Collection
A0747 Skyline